CONTENTS

GET ON THE WATER!

Are you ready for an adventure on water? Wherever you live, you are not far from the water, whether it is a river, a lake, a lagoon or even the sea. Kayaking and canoeing are amazing fun and great ways to connect with nature.

Kayaks and canoes are both narrow, shallow boats that you propel with a **paddle**. The main difference between them is how they are paddled.

A kayak paddle is long and has a **blade** (the flat part that you pull through the water) at both ends. A canoe paddle is shorter, with a blade at just one end. There is more room for gear in a canoe and they tend to be more stable. Kayaks are easier to paddle solo and can generally go faster.

A kayak or canoe can take you places you would not normally see.

4

Both kayaks and canoes can be paddled by one person or two.

The best way to start canoeing or kayaking is to learn the basic skills from an instructor before you head downstream. You will find help at your local kayaking and canoeing club. The club may offer kayak and canoe rentals, classes and even kayaking and canoeing holidays. Whether you want to quietly explore a lake or river or pit your skills against others in a competition, there is something for everyone in this exciting water sport.

PLAN YOUR TRIP

To make the most of your kayaking or canoeing trip, you need to do some planning in advance. If you have thought about where you are going, the weather conditions and, importantly, the water conditions, you will have a great trip.

Canoeing or kayaking in the river is different throughout the year. In summer, rivers usually have less water in them and flow more slowly. The sun can burn, however, and there is a risk of dehydration if you do not drink plenty of water. In spring, it is great to see nature reawakening and in the autumn the colours are beautiful. At these times of year, you will need warm clothing.

Whenever you go on your trip, it is important to find out about the water conditions. You do not want to set off down a gentle river only to find yourself on a ride through the rapids downstream! Your local kayaking shop is a good place to get advice about the best locations.

Take a canoe out on a lake at different times of the year and see the landscape change with the seasons.

Kayaking at sea brings more challenges from the waves and the currents.

STAY SAFE!

Water can be dangerous. Before you start kayaking or canoeing, you must know how to swim.

A lake is a great place for beginners because it is much less likely to hold surprises than rivers or the sea. If you have more experience, you can hit the waves and take your kayak out on the sea. Sea kayaking is more risky than kayaking on a lake. The sea is full of water **currents** that can carry you in directions you do not want to go, so this type of kayaking is definitely not for beginners.

GET THE GEAR

You can rent a kayak, canoe and paddles until you are sure you want to buy your own. Whether you rent or buy your equipment, having the right clothing and other gear from the start of your trip will make it much safer and more fun.

First, you need to organize your clothes. You need to wear the right clothing to be comfortable as you kayak or canoe. Even on a hot day, the water can be pretty cold. If it gets through your clothes, you will feel cold and uncomfortable. Keep warm with a wetsuit or a waterproof suit with sealed cuffs. Add warm clothes underneath the waterproof suit for chilly days. Gloves are a good idea, too, as wet hands can get very cold. Last of all, you will need waterproof shoes.

wetsuit

life jacket

spray skirt

Always wear waterproof clothing.

The buoyancy aid is the single most important piece of equipment you need.

Your helmet should cover the sides of your head and the back of your neck and fit well. Keep it buckled!

In a kayak, another great piece of gear is the spray deck. This goes around your waist and attaches to the rim of the **cockpit**, to keep the water out of the boat. You will want a dry bag, too, to carry items such as a first aid kit, water, phone, whistle and dry clothes. The bag should attach securely to the boat.

Safety is a major concern on the water. You must wear a **buoyancy aid** such as a life jacket, to help you float if you fall in. Always protect your head with a helmet. Riverbanks and beds can be rocky, and if you **capsize** you could hit your head. A helmet is a must if you are tackling fast-flowing water.

9

KAYAKS AND CANOES

When you are starting out, you will probably use a basic kayak or canoe. However, there are many different boat shapes and designs. Some are designed for speed, and some for stability. As you become more confident, choose the best one for the type of canoeing or kayaking you want to do.

One of the key design features in the boat is the shape of the bottom, or **keel**. A flat bottom makes the boat easy to turn quickly, but it is also less stable because it tips over easily and it is harder to balance in. Flat-bottomed kayaks are therefore generally used for **white water** or fast-flowing conditions. A V-shaped keel makes the kayak more stable but harder to turn, so it is better for beginners.

STAY SAFE!

If you are new to the sport, use a two-person canoe or kayak with an adult.

The open design of the canoe makes it ideal for using on calmer water.

The pointed ends of these two kayaks make it easier to move in rough water.

The width and length of the boat are important, too. Long, narrow kayaks are more **streamlined** than shorter ones. This means they will keep moving through the water for longer after each stroke. These kayaks are also designed for touring, which makes them ideal if you are going a long distance. Canoes are wider than kayaks, and less suited to long distances. They are also open-topped, so they are better for calm conditions when water is less likely to get in.

Paddles can be made of wood, metal or plastic. Choose a paddle that is light and strong, so that it is not too tiring to use. Canoe paddles are more likely to be made of wood than kayak paddles, because they are smaller and lighter.

Kayak paddles have a blade at each end. They are light but strong.

11

GET READY

You have got the gear, you have chosen your boat and you are ready to go to the water. Now you need to master some important skills to get safely afloat.

Kayaks and canoes are heavy, but if you learn how to carry them properly you will not hurt yourself. For a canoe, you will definitely need two people to carry it. Take one end of the boat each. Kayaks often have loops at each end to make it easy for two people to carry them. If you are carrying a kayak alone, put your arm inside it and slowly lift it up onto your shoulder. Make sure that your back takes most of the weight.

Your back, not your shoulder, should take the boat's weight.

SITTING PROPERLY

To stop your muscles from becoming sore, learn how to sit correctly in your kayak before you put it in the water!

1 Carefully get into the boat, sit down and make sure you are comfortable.

2 Adjust the back support so that you are not leaning backwards. Your chest should be slightly forwards.

3 Place the balls of your feet on the footrests, with your toes pointing outwards.

4 Adjust the footrests so that your knees are pointing upwards and outwards. Your legs should be in contact with the thigh braces on the kayak.

5 Rock the kayak from side to side, and lean backwards and forwards, to make sure you are comfortable. You should feel at one with the boat.

If you sit in the correct position, you will have a comfortable ride.

LAUNCHING

Even the most experienced kayakers and canoeists sometimes find it hard to get into and launch their boats. With practice and balance, though, you can make sure you do not get too wet!

You can launch a canoe or kayak from a beach, a jetty or a riverbank. The technique is different for each location. It is best to practice in shallow water first, to perfect your balancing skills. Once you are confident, you can try launching from other locations. Some kayakers can launch from a steep riverbank or jetty. Firstly, they get in the boat, then they lean backwards as the kayak dips down into the water. Canoes cannot be launched this way because they would fill up with water!

Launching from a beach into shallow water is best for beginners.

14

LAUNCH OFF!

Follow these steps to launch a kayak from a shallow riverbank or jetty.

1 Put the kayak in the shallow water and stand alongside it.

2 Rest the paddle on the deck behind the cockpit, with one end still resting on the bank.

3 Grip the paddle at the edge of the cockpit with one hand. This will help to steady you as you climb into the boat.

4 Carefully climb in. Sit on the back of the cockpit first, then slide your bottom in.

5 Fasten the spray deck if you are using one.

6 Bring the paddle around in front of you and then use it to push away from the bank.

EXPLORE THIS!

You will need:
- kayak
- paddle
- spray deck (optional)

Start paddling as you move away from the bank.

USE YOUR PADDLES

It may sound odd, but there is a right way and a wrong way to hold the paddle when you are kayaking or canoeing. If you hold your paddle incorrectly, you will put a strain on your body.

Most people hold a kayak paddle backwards the first time they pick it up. However, this is incorrect and will result in less power in your stroke. Your paddle blade has a smooth side and a ridged side. Keep the smooth side facing you. This is the side to pull through the water.

The middle of the paddle is the **shaft**. If you are right-handed, grip it in your right hand. This is your control grip, so it needs to be firm but not too tight. The other hand grips less tightly and slips around as you paddle on each side. Make sure that your hands are centred on the paddle and are a little wider apart than your shoulders.

Make strokes on alternate sides of the boat to go straight forwards.

STAY SAFE!

In a canoe, swap arms so that each arm takes a turn. This avoids putting stress on just one arm.

It is most efficient to paddle on the left side of the canoe when your right hand is on top of the paddle.

When canoeing, start by bringing your top hand up above your head, so that the shaft is almost vertical. Reach forwards and put the blade in the water, keeping it upright. Pull with your bottom hand, and push with your top hand. This will move the blade in a straight line.

Once you have mastered moving forwards, you can start to learn how to change direction and turn around. To turn your canoe or kayak you use the forwards and backwards strokes and a stroke called the "sweep stroke".

The sweep stroke turns the boat away from the side on which you use it. Twist away from that side, then put the blade in the water up by the **bow**. Use your core muscles to twist and turn the boat around the blade. Remove the blade from the water when it gets to the **stern**. To make a sharp turn, take a backwards stroke. This is the forwards stroke in reverse.

To turn around, paddle on only one side of the boat.

DRAW STROKE

You will need to use the **"draw stroke"** to move your boat sideways in the water, such as towards a bank. You use the same stroke for both kayaking and canoeing.

You will need:
- kayak or canoe
- paddle

1 Twist at the waist to face the direction in which you wish to move. If you want to move right, twist right. If you want to move left, twist left.

2 Reach out towards the water with the paddle blade. Your left hand should be at about eye level.

3 Put the paddle in the water as far from the boat as you can. It should be facing the side of the boat.

4 Pull the blade in towards the boat, but not touching the side.

5 Rotate the blade out of the water, towards the stern.

6 Repeat the stroke until you reach your destination.

STAY SAFE!

Do not push on the paddle when using a draw stroke, or you may capsize.

A draw stroke is used to move the boat sideways.

21

A QUICK EXIT

Being out on the water can be dangerous. You need to know how to get out of your kayak quickly if it overturns and you find yourself in the water.

First, you will need to know how to keep yourself upright if your kayak starts to wobble. A "**brace stroke**" will get you straight when you are slightly overbalanced on one side. Sit upright holding the paddle. While keeping your hands low, lift your elbows almost to your shoulders. Keep your head over the boat. Lift the paddle on the side nearest the water, then bring the paddle down hard, flat onto the water surface. Flick yourself upright from the hips.

If you are starting to overbalance, a brace stroke can get you upright again.

It is essential to master your wet-exit from a kayak before you go on the river. Ask for help from an instructor or buddy.

If you overturn your kayak, do not panic! Bring your body close to the deck. In other words, tuck yourself forwards. This protects you from underwater obstacles and makes it easier to get your legs out of the kayak. Pull the toggle on the spray deck to detach it. Push the kayak up, forwards and away from your legs. Make sure you grab your paddle when you come back to the surface. Swim to your kayak and hold it. Stay with it if you can, but the most important thing is to get to shore safely.

STAY SAFE!

If you are separated from your kayak or canoe, avoid underwater obstacles such as rocks or roots by floating on your back with your hands crossed over your chest.

23

WHITE WATER

White-water kayaking or canoeing is the wildest experience you can have on the water. If you are brave enough to try it, it can be incredible!

White water is water that is full of air. It froths, churns and swirls down-river very quickly. It is made white by rushing over rocks and other obstacles below the surface. These are a hazard for the paddler. White-water rivers are graded from one to six, according to how hard and dangerous they are to paddle down. Even an expert paddler would find a grade six river a serious challenge.

Experienced paddlers can read the river for the safest course to take.

White-water canoeists in a **slalom** competition follow a twisting course between pairs of poles, or "gates".

White-water rivers can be narrow and deep, or broad and full of torrents. Before setting out, research the conditions you are likely to find. Ask experienced paddlers and look in books and on the internet. It is essential to master the strokes necessary to control your boat through the conditions you find. Experts also learn to "read" the surface of the river for what lies beneath. For example, V-shaped ripples pointing upstream are a sign of rocks below, so always avoid those. A **chute** is an area of smooth water in a white-water section and is usually the safest route through.

READY TO ROLL

When you are white-water kayaking or canoeing, you are much more likely to capsize. There are several things you can do if this happens, but you will need to practise them before you take to any white water.

You have hit a problem and you are about to capsize. With experience you will learn how to "hip-snap" your boat back upright before you capsize. This uses your hips and core body muscles. If you have gone under, you must make a split-second decision whether to exit your kayak underwater or stay in it. Ideally, you turn the boat back upright without getting out.

If you exit, you can lose the kayak and paddle and will have to swim through dangerous water. You might be able to do a **"buddy roll"**, in which another kayak comes to your capsized boat. You hold onto the boat and pull yourself back upright.

If you overbalance too far, you will go under!

ESKIMO ROLL

The "**Eskimo roll**" is a technique that a kayaker can use to turn over his or her kayak without getting out of it.

1 Capsize the boat so that you are upside down in the water.

2 Bring your head and body forwards so that you are as close to the boat as possible.

3 Position your paddle alongside the kayak, and reach your hands out of the water as high as you can.

4 Turn the paddle across the kayak bottom and reach your top arm as far over the kayak as possible.

5 Reach out with the lower arm to get the outer blade up to the surface.

6 Keep your head down on the shoulder of your lower arm.

7 Hip-snap back upright, pushing down on the paddle blade at the same time.

8 Stabilize yourself and do not lift your head up too quickly.

You will need:

- kayak • paddle
- calm, safe water or pool to practise in

STAY SAFE!

You must only attempt an Eskimo roll under adult supervision.

Every white-water kayaker will flip over at some time. The Eskimo roll is an essential skill to master.

27

GO GREEN

We all have a responsibility to keep our countryside safe and unspoilt for the future. That way, everyone can continue to enjoy it. Whatever your outdoor adventure, remember to respect the natural environment and try to make as little impact on it as you can.

Our rivers, lakes and seas are beautiful, and kayakers and canoeists need to keep them that way. If you are going on a canoeing adventure upriver or exploring a lake, never drop anything into the water. Litter can seriously harm fish, birds and other creatures living in or by the water. They might eat it or get tangled in it. Litter pollutes the water, too.

If you stop for a picnic or to camp on the bank, make sure that you pack up your litter and take it home with you. Be aware that some creatures make their homes on the riverbank. Do not get too close or disturb parents and their young with your boat.

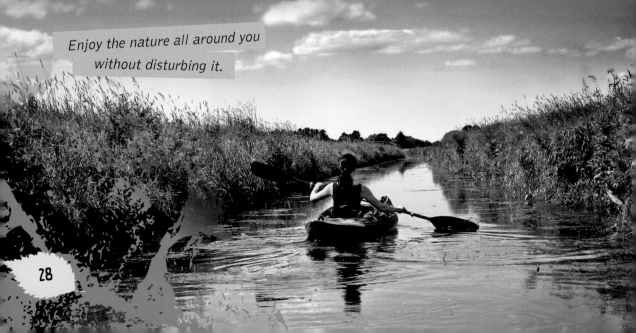

Enjoy the nature all around you without disturbing it.

Make sure you take home everything you brought on your trip.

If you are an experienced kayaker or canoeist and you enjoy launching directly from a steep bank or rocks, think about the terrain you are on. Be careful not to damage the wildlife around your boat. White-water paddling is more likely to threaten you than the wildlife, but try to grab your gear if you capsize and wet-exit. That way you will not leave it to pollute the water.

GLOSSARY

blade wide, flat part at the end of a paddle

bow front end of a kayak or canoe

brace stroke paddling stroke that helps you to stay upright after tilting to one side

buddy roll help from someone in another canoe to flip you back upright after capsizing

buoyancy aid inflated waterproof jacket that helps you to float in water

capsize turn over so that you are in the water

chute path of smooth, fast-flowing water

cockpit open part of a kayak that you sit in

current movement in a body of water that can be fast-moving and unpredictable

draw stroke paddling stroke that moves a kayak or canoe sideways

Eskimo roll technique for getting back upright in a kayak after capsizing, without getting out

keel underside of a boat

paddle equipment used to propel a kayak or canoe, with a long handle, or shaft, and a blade at either one end or both ends

shaft part of the paddle that you hold on to

slalom event in which kayak or canoe racers navigate a series of gates along a white-water course

stern back end of a kayak or canoe

streamlined shaped to move efficiently through the water

sweep stroke paddling stroke used for turning and steering

wet-exit technique for getting out of a kayak underwater after capsizing

white water fast-moving, turbulent water

FIND OUT MORE

Books

Canoeing and Kayaking (Get Outdoors), Lois Rock (Wayland, 2012)

Canoeing and Other Water Sports (Clever Clogs), Jason Page (Ticktock, 2008)

Scouting Skills (A Complete Guide), Various (Doubleday Childrens, 2010)

Wild Water: Canoeing and Kayaking (Adventure Outdoors), Neil Champion (Franklin Watts, 2012)

Websites

www.gocanoeing.org.uk/go/index.cfm/hints-tips/buying-a-canoe-or-kayak
Learn all about the types of kayak available with helpful hints and tips about which kayak may suit you.

www.gocanoeing.org.uk/go/index.cfm/hints-tips/safety-advice/fish-olympics
Discover how to look after yourself, your equipment and your environment when out canoeing or kayaking.

www.onthewater.co.uk/which_activity/paddle_powered/kayaking/where_to_kayak.aspx
Find out where in the United Kingdom you can kayak, and look up information on how to get a licence.

INDEX